Endorsement

Inspiration and collaboration are evident in Sheldon Clark's and George Keltika's engaging volume of poetry and prayer sketches. The subject matter includes religious themes, human desire, lullaby, prayer, and perspective on the future and the immediate. Mr. Keltika's black and white sketches are artistic metaphors, which open light to each of the poems. It has been a joy to hear Sheldon read his poetry and to talk with him about the back stories the poetic muses placed in front of him on his poetic journey.

Charlotte Washington
Business Performance Management, Mohawk College
Resident Service Coordinator/Administration, Highgate Residence

Previous Publications by Sheldon H. Clark

Voices Extended (with Neil Paul), 2013
Still Voices, 2020, 2021

Preface

Poetry and Prayer Sketches grew out of a graduate course offered at the Earlham School of Religion, by Susanna Childress in Richmond, Indiana, during the Spring Term of 2008. The sketches were the result of conversations with a long time friend, George S. Keltika, who had just retired from teaching Art at Pickering College, Newmarket, Ontario, where we had been colleagues for many years.

The purpose of this booklet is to use it as a springboard for discussions about religion, poetry and literature. Participants may enjoy puzzling over the biblical allusions and documenting them in chapter and verse. Others might enjoy exploring the poetic references, finding them, and then reading the original poems. Certainly, questions should be raised about the relationship between the prayers, poems and sketches. For example:

- What is the story?
- What is the philosophical point?
- What did the artist see and hear in the words that perhaps inspired his interpretation?
- Does the sketch enhance the meaning of the poem or prayer?
- Do the poems and prayers enhance the meaning of the sketches?
- What is the creative tension found between a particular writing and its sketch?
- How do the poems, prayers and sketches enlarge one's vision?

Poetry and Prayer Sketches is an invitation to share with others echoes that spark happiness and thoughtfulness in the Light.

Sheldon H. Clark, D. Min.

Published by
Rock's Mills Press
www.rocksmillspress.com

Copyright © 2008, 2013 by Sheldon H. Clark (words)
Copyright © 2013 by George H. Keltika (artwork)
All rights reserved. Reproduction in whole or in part without the express written permission of the copyright holder is prohibited.

Table of Contents

Pebbles……………………………………………………………………………………. 6
Soul Is…………………………………………………………………………………….. 8
The Child…………………………………………………………………………………. 10
The Want I Want………………………………………………………………………… 12
Someone Opens an Orange in Silence……………………………………………… 14
The Moon Leans Like This……………………………………………………………. 16
Trinity, Plus One………………………………………………………………………… 18
Accept Me………………………………………………………………………………… 20
Almighty God, Giver of Life……………………………………………………………. 22
Leviathans, Cranberry Shore, Vinalhaven, Maine………………………………….. 24
Loving Imperatives……………………………………………………………………… 26
A Prayer…………………………………………………………………………………… 28

Pebbles

Dear God,
We remember before you this day
The pebbles upon which Christ trod.

Those pebbles which supported Jew and non-Jew,
Free people, and slaves,
Civilians and soldiers of the Roman Legions.

The pebbles are separated by dust.
The dust from which, it is written, we are born
The dust which supported His feet.

The pebbles are mighty in their silence.
The pebbles support me.
The dust is stirred by my feet.

I follow His feet, His body.
I walk on His pebbles.
I desire to follow wherever He may lead.

Dear God,
Broken, fallen, stumbling always moving,
Walking the walk.
The silent, mighty, dusty pebbles,
Ageless friends,
Meet our steps.

Thanksgiving and praise for the pebbles,
For the dust for the dust for the dust
For each of our steps in His steps.

Amen.

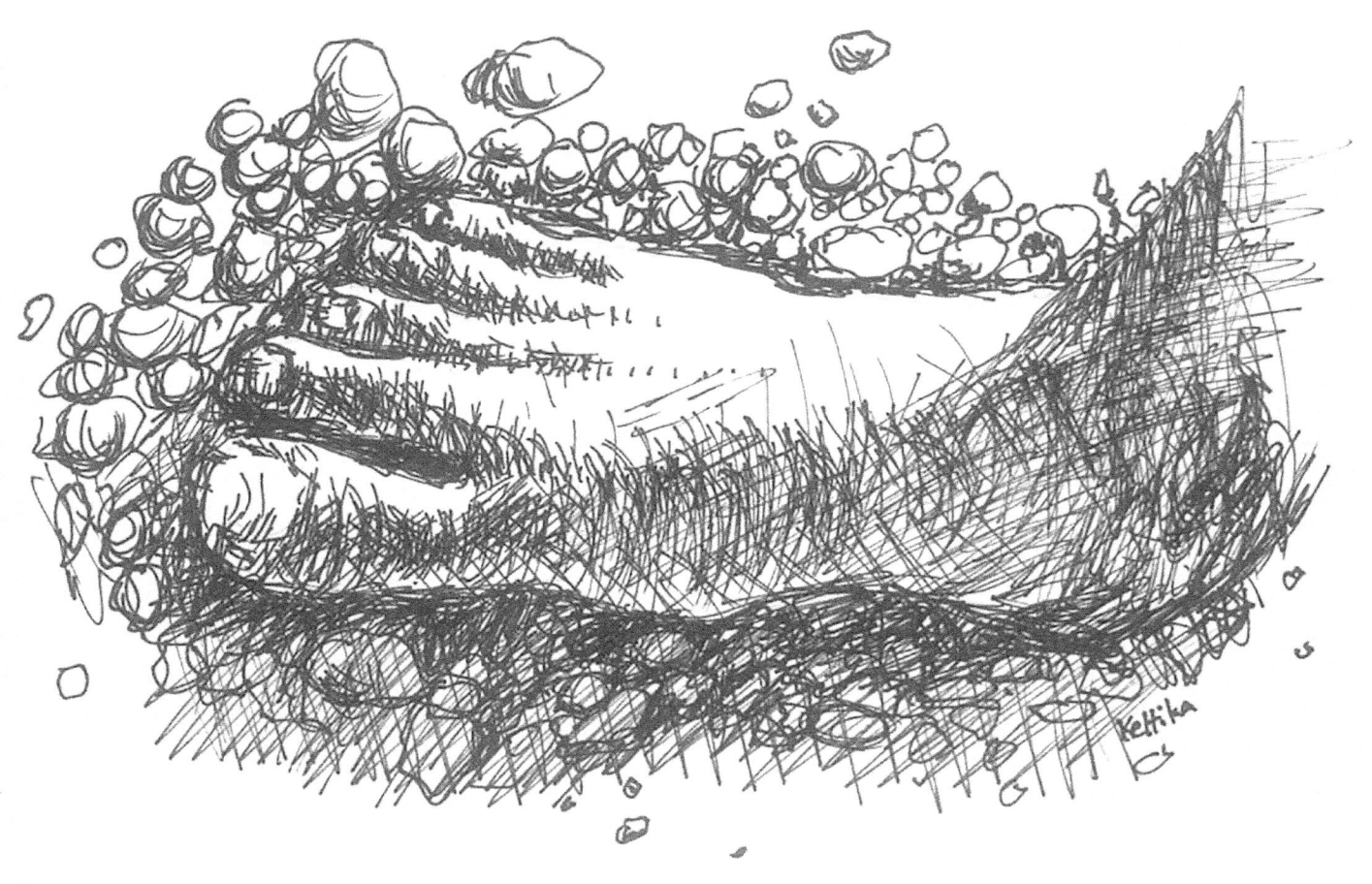

Soul Is

Soul: *"Spiritual essence of being"*

Soul is

An open circle,

A cross within,

Beyond poles,

Beyond equators.

Soul. Soul.

Our outer shell,

Our material form

Simply cannot contain the essence of **Soul.**

The form within

Simply cannot contain the essence of **Soul.**

Paradoxically, **Soul** is within outstretched arms,

The Spiritual, non-dimensional intersection of the cross,

And way beyond the confines of any spherical limitations.

Imagination is the liberating instrument

For the infiniteness of **Soul.**

Soul. Soul. Soul.

The Child

The child actually knew.
Amazed elders with rote-learned groans
Grew into the ever-widening circle of silent
Attention, question, and awe.

The child actually knew.
Truly, really, without disguise
Silent-sounds, innocent-knowledge
Life-death, knowledge-wisdom
Comprehension beyond memory.

The child actually knew.
Mother-parent, father-parent
Brothers, sisters, all
Related by life's
Eternal light displays
Knew Grandeur.

The child taught them
As one having authority.
Beyond age, Ages, apprenticeships, book-learned
Tight-fisted brokered deals,
Devil's knowledge,
Alpha, omega.

The child became
Grace
Made by passion.

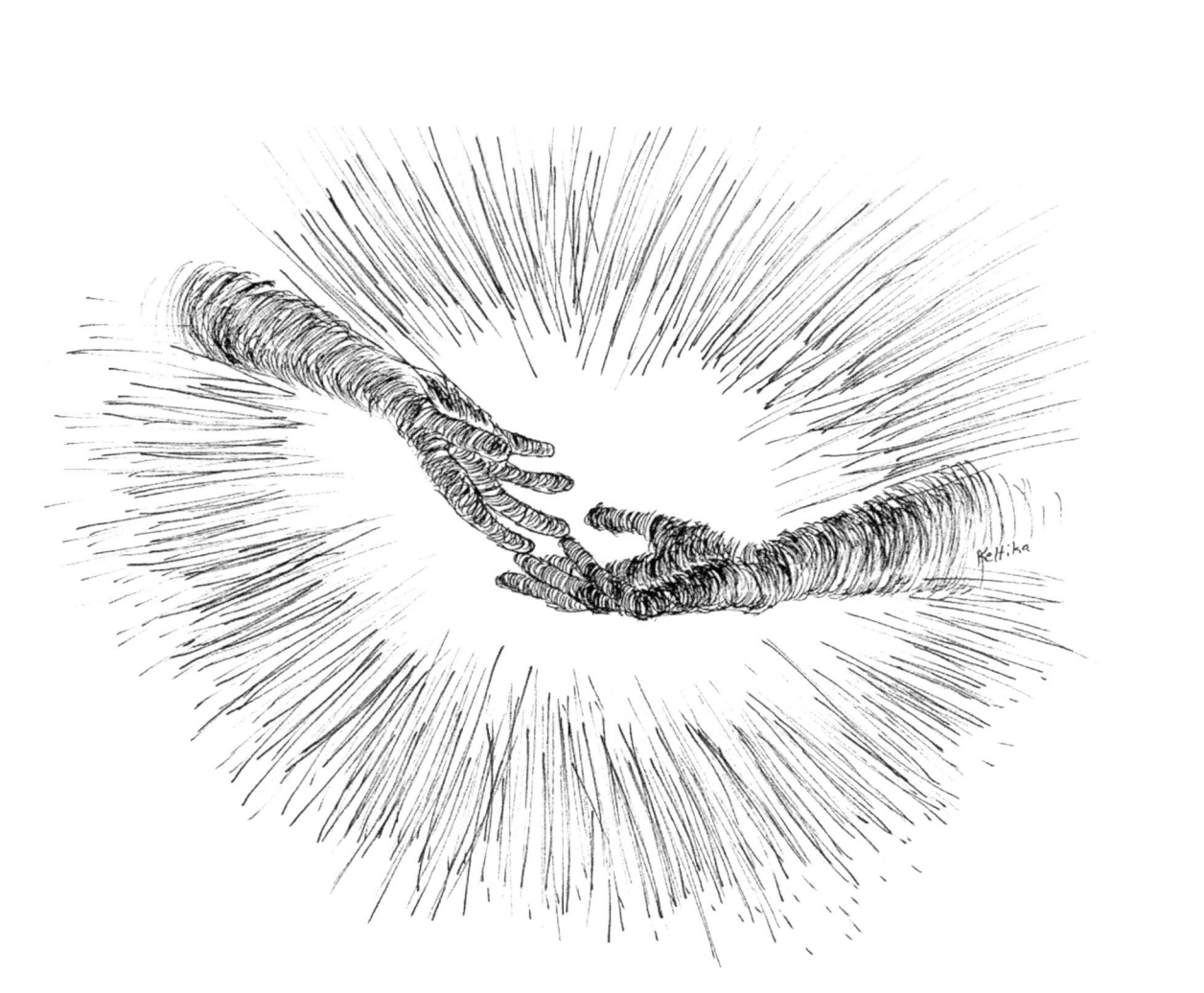

The Want I Want

The want I want is want from what want demands.

The want I want is want from poverty, hunger, injustice, and basic needs.
The want I want is want from physical sickness, mental sickness, and Spiritual disease.
The want I want is want from lies, innuendo, falsehoods, half-truths.

Wealth and poverty, nothing and plenty, excess and deprivation,
Even-Stephen unfairness, infinite much and finite little, all want.
Bodies, minds, souls, want.
Food, clothing, shelter wants fill nomadic meanderings across deserts
To mountaintops,
Down into the shadows of evil.

Search wants John and Jane Doe's wherever, whenever, forever.

Loss wants to be found.
Grief wants to end.
Death, itself, is transfigured by want.
God and the Devil want.

The want-lists want obedience, innocence, loyalty, dedication, creation,
Atmospheres, black holes, quantitative analysis, dimensions, erasures,
Opportunities, hopefulness, kindness, friendship, instinct, order, randomness,
And especially faith, hope, and love.

The want-lists are not wanting for want.

They are the endless identifications of what could be.
If only
The insatiable could become sated
And put an end
To want.

Someone Opens an Orange in Silence

Someone opens an orange in silence at a sidewalk cafe.

She cradles the globed fruit with loving hands,
folded umbilical looking out expectantly, and
Cointreau induced saliva
moistened lips,
prepare.

Human apertures
gently separate the engorged skin,
reveal the hidden core,
the emerging freshness
Nature does the rest.

Juice squirts its tenderness without–
within a tissue tears to release
the half, the quarter, the crescent moons.

This *ménage à deux*,
is as slow steady silent
as the birthing of a foal at midnight.

Wet hands lift newborn fruit to tongue
to taste to emulsify to ingest in God's sweet order.

Politely, passersby avert their eyes,
curious
to smell to touch to taste
to hear to see
Someone who opens an orange in silence.

The Moon Leans Like This

And the moon leans like this off to one side,
not perfectly positioned,
but present pronounced secure.

And the moon leans like this to one side, elliptical oval light shadow,
and beaming a muted ray.

The moon leans like this, reclining
to share the bed time story, the pillow,
Comfortable and loving.

The moon leans like this
arching, stretching, yawning, sighing
to the bye-baby-bunting who takes
but a single breath, and then,
sleeps behind a cloud.

Trinity, Plus One

Clusters offered, I selected,
passed the plate
and held in front
a trinity, plus one.

Placed, assembled,
the three, plus one, resembled
Newton's First Law of Motion
"An object at rest will remain at rest."

A triad of almost spheroids rest together,
like uneven marbles in a small bowl.
Odd Man Out, the other, placed pointedly,
imposition, as it were.

No sweet succulent temptations
second time 'round
to single out, rearrange, contrast, colour,
shape, size, smell, bite.

My trinity plus one, and pulp,
held firm as suntan over lounging muscles,
bare-naked, teasing by revealing
what was to come,

First, one triune sacrificed,
the second offered, given, and then,
the last element, communed.
The palate insatiable sighed, "One more."

Odd Man Out, waited, rested (Newton)
The moment of truth.
Trinity, plus one, lifted, suspended, devoured,
Communed.

Accept Me

Accept me.
Love me.
Forgive me.

Accept me as I am.
Love me, as I am, toes to head and down again.
Forgive my trespasses.
Show justice, mercy, humility.

Accept me.
Love me.
Forgive me.

Accept my race, creed, colour,
Caucasian, Mongolian, Negroid, outer space,
White, brown, yellow, aqua marine,
This ism, that ism, and other isms that isms make.

Accept me.
Love me.
Forgive me.

Love me simply for the fact, I am.
Love me for the truth, you are.
Love me, as I am alone, and we are together.
Love without tenses.

Accept me.
Love me.
Forgive me.

Forgive me. Justice is peace.
Forgive me. Mercy is everlasting.
Forgive me. Truth endures.

Accept me.
Love me.
Forgive me.

Almighty God, Giver of Life

Thank you, Almighty God, Giver of Life,
For this life.
Given. Received.
Conceived. Birthed.
Pray with us now and in the hour of our need.

Thank you,
For the gift of this moment.
Love, life, eternity are as
Close as wick and flame, meniscus and ether.
I am lost in a world of inconsistency and intrigue.
And yet, the moon and the sun
Continue to pursue each other.
Where does one leave off, the other begin?
Your Spirit shepherd crooks us across the chasms.

Thank you,
For the moment in which lovers face their beloved,
Hearts beat to heart beats, prayers to pray-ers.
I find myself wondering, wandering, praying,
Helpless in your arms, a poor sinner in the
Arms of an angel held by Grace.

Amen.

Leviathans, Cranberry Shore, Vinalhaven, Maine

Me, proud father, took a snap one foggy day
of Amber, Cranberry Shore, Vinalhaven, Maine, where
ghosting within the North Atlantic's impossible horizon
tall ships drifted from somewhere to someplace else.

The photo is of a six-year old, two tall mast pine, pea soup fog, and
rock, seaweed, sending up memory smells of
fish-death and life emerging from the saltiness.

Leviathan smooth bedrock decorated the shorelines tide out,
Viewers redirect their eyes side-to-side
up-and-beyond sail to sail to sail to sail
and the winking line of the sky reaching water reaching sky.
This day the doldrums sea sprite is a shroud that opens and closes
vision and vision.

Along the shore the eyes respond,
a blond-blue dot kneeling in front of a hidden pool without a care.
No tidal threat foreseen. No schooners spooking in the fog.
Discovery waits right in front of that ledge, this one, right here:
water-strider, crab shell, barnacles, dead fish, minnows, and some
sparkle deep down there.

Yesterday was. Tomorrow shall be. *Carpe Diem*.
Today is the day, to live to love to be at one.

My photographer's shutter preserves this moment
recorded more by luck than by design,
and yet, design it is.
Muted tones black, blue, white, green, reds, grays, three dimensions in two,
a leviathan morning in Maine.

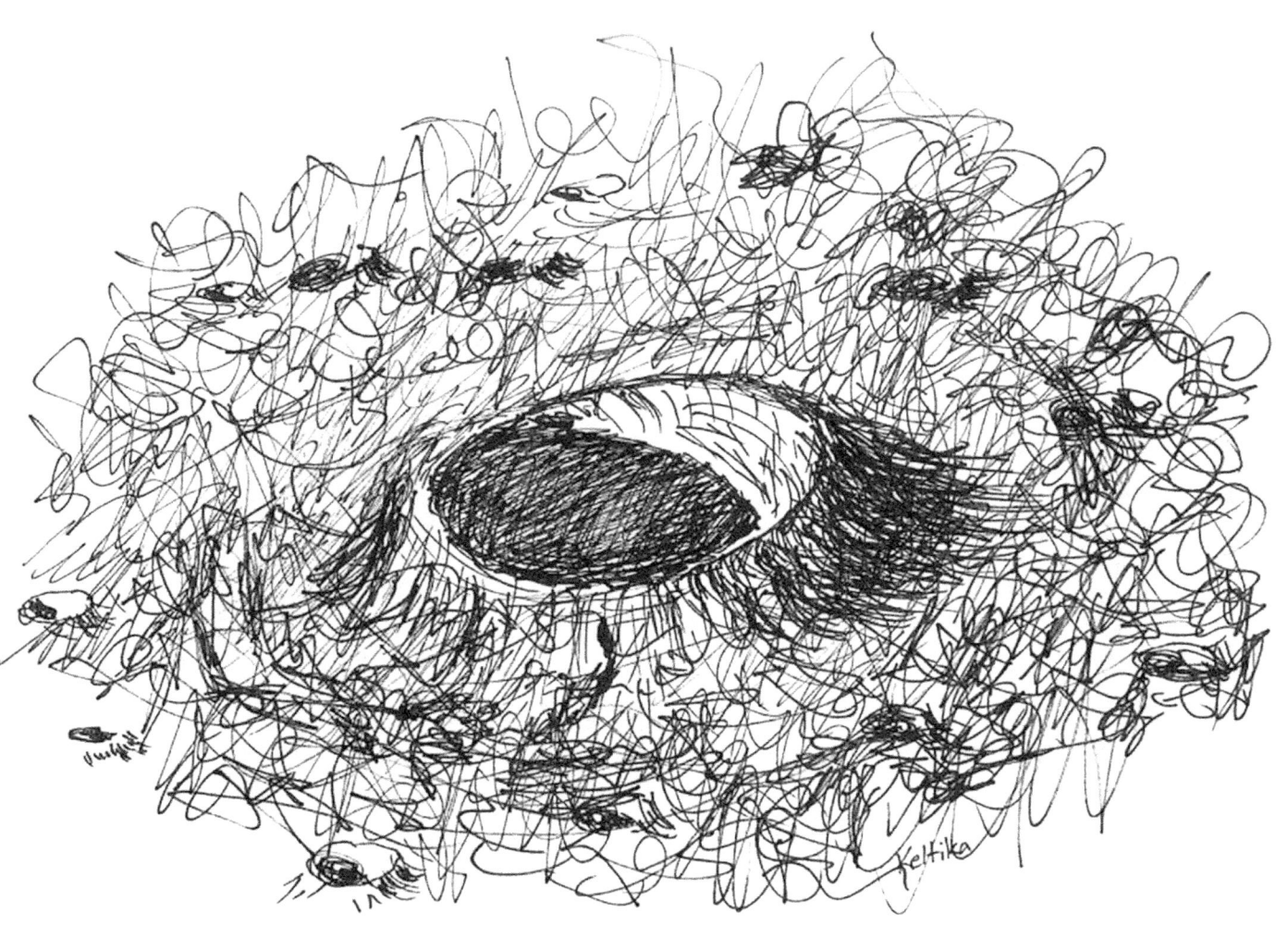

Loving Imperatives

Children, I warn you to love deeply
as you slip in and out of babyhood, adolescence,
youthful playfulness, adulthood,
and so-called maturity.
To every age there is a season.

Children, I warn you to love what you do
To do whatever it is well, exactly, with the same attention to detail,
the same precision
God brought to Eden.
Love creation as God did.

Children, I warn you to love to study from life itself;
hot coals, migration patterns, sharp knives, the sea, the soft folds
of mother's father's lover's warmth, laughter, intensity.
Hop, skip and jump leaping into the pool, the jungle, the desert, the city of measurement.
Cultivate the body.

Children, I warn you to love classical studies.
Read, write, speak well in an informed way,
gentle, kindly, but with conviction and certitude, and
after deep thought share with others.
Cultivate the mind.

Children, I warn you to love the experience of the fullness of life,
but not at the expense of life itself, where bit-by-bit
one is destroyed
by careless pride-filled-selfishness.
Cultivate the spirit.

Children, I warn you to love to delve deep.
Reach beyond your grasp. Keep the Golden Rule.
Love God and your neighbor as yourself.
Grow to love your unique irreplaceable you.
In God's image you are made.

Children, I warn you.

A Prayer

Dear God help me.
I am lost in a world of inconsistency and intrigue.
Who isn't?
I value honesty and integrity.
Who doesn't?
Where does one leave off and the other begin?
Does it really matter?
What are the lines?
Lines and squares? Watch out for the bears!
Inconsistency? Honesty?
Who wait in the corners for the sillies.
Intrigue? Integrity?
Who step where they shouldn't.
Are these poles? Flip sides of the same coin?
The equator goes 'round the world in one big embrace.
Something quite different? Quite apart?
A star?

I love deeply, profoundly, consistently, and honestly.
Eventide waxes and wanes as the moon.
Wherein lies guile? cynicism? happenstance? situation?
Venus? Nokomis? Daughter of the moon? Nokomis.
I am seeking truth. Who reveals Truth to whom?
God! The Divine Spark. The Supreme Being.
What is the frame?
Eternity. A lifetime can be eternity. So can the moment.
Death is so near, so close, so much a matter of moment.
Thank you, God, mother, father, for the gift of life. Here, gone.
The tick tick, lub dub of a heart beat.
Steady. White on green. Constant. Without a flicker.
Silence. Silence. Silence. Silence. Silence. Silence. Silence.
Hands 'round the bed.

"It is all right to let go." Peace.
I am a monk at prayer. Silent.
Ages of prayers have been witnesses for me, now,
Prostrate upon the stone. Face toward the altar. Silence.
In the hour of our need.

"Dear God help me."
I am a lover. Face toward beloved. Silence.
Embrace is as close to Salvation as I'll ever be.
Hear my heart beat. Listen to my breath. Hear my prayer.
"I am yours, my love, my inspiration, my muse, my adoration."
"I love you." "I accept you." "I forgive you."
Even as God loves, accepts and forgives the least, for I am he.
I need love, acceptance, forgiveness.
The death of innocence is the birth of knowledge.
We are so young, so old, so a part of eternity.
Today is our day. Yesterday is but a dusty shadow.
Apart. Together. The part of the Eternal connected.
Now. Here and now is right for being and becoming.
I am lost wondering, wandering, praying, helpless.
I am found in your arms, a poor sinner with an angel.

Amen.

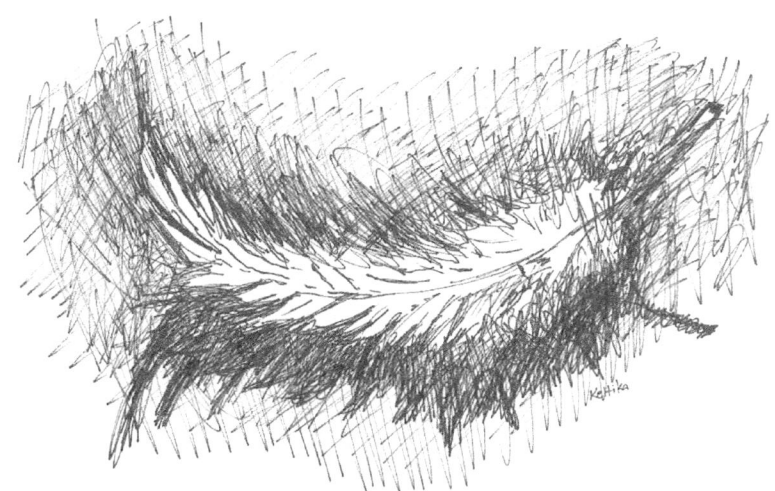

www.ingramcontent.com/pod-product-compliance
Lightning Source LLC
LaVergne TN
LVHW081528060526
838200LV00045B/2041